PRACTICAL FISHKEEPING

SEAHORSES

Neil Garrick-Maidment

Neil Garrick-Maidment

RINGPRESS

ABOUT THE AUTHOR

Neil Garrick-Maidment is a Seahorse specialist, who has enjoyed great success at breeding Seahorses in captivity. Neil set up the Seahorse Trust, in Devon, which promotes Seahorse conservation and education, and, in 1994, he launched the British Seahorse Survey, to discover approximate numbers and locations of British species.

www.theseahorsetrust.co.uk

SCIENTIFIC CONSULTANT: Dr. Peter Burgess BSc, MSc, MPhil, PhD is an experienced aquarium hobbyist and international consultant on ornamental fish.

Commercial products shown in this book are for illustrative purposes only and are not necessarily endorsed by the author.

Photography: Francis Apesteguy (p.15, p.16, p.21, p.26, p.37, p.51, p.39, p.55, p.58), Neil Garrick-Maidment (main cover image, p.18, p.19) and Brian Garrick (p.49, p.54). All other photos by Keith Allison and courtesy of Tetra UK.
Line drawings: Viv Rainsbury
Picture editor: Claire Horton-Bussey
Design: Rob Benson

Note: photos showing Seahorses and seafans together are purely for photographic decorative purposes only – and are not recommended for general Seahorse-keeping.

**Published by Ringpress Books,
a division of Interpet Publishing,**
Vincent Lane, Dorking, Surrey, RH4 3YX, UK
Tel: 01306 873822   Fax: 01306 876712
email: sales@interpet.co.uk

First published 2002
© 2002 Ringpress Books. All rights reserved

ISBN 1 86054 265 4

Printed and bound in Hong Kong through
Printworks International Ltd.

10 9 8 7 6 5 4 3 2 1

CONTENTS

CHAPTER 1

WHAT IS A SEAHORSE?

What a curious fish the Seahorse is; it defies logic as to why nature assembled so many parts of other animals together into one. It is not until you look closely at this remarkable fish – and it is a true fish – that you begin to realise how superbly designed it is for its environment.

MONKEY TAIL

The Seahorse's most unfish-like feature is the tail. Being prehensile, it is more like a monkey's tail than a fish's. The tail seems to have a mind of its own, sometimes grabbing at the nearest piece of weed without telling its owner, who is then brought to a sudden halt, quite often bashing the slender tube snout against the weed.

SEAHORSE SNOUT

The elongated snout is part of the head of the Seahorse, and it is this feature which gives the Seahorse its name – due to the resemblance to a horse's head.

The Seahorse's prehensile 'monkey-like' tail is strong and flexible.

SEAHORSE ANATOMY

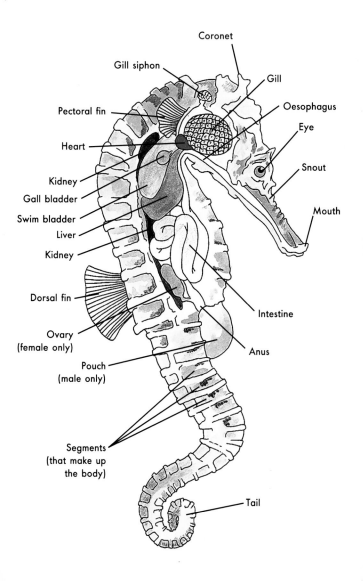

The snout also gives the Seahorse its Latin family name of Sygnathidae, which means 'fused tube'.

The snout consists of several plates fused together to form the tube through which the Seahorse sucks its prey (food). This is done with such force that it disintegrates the food, ready for eating as it is sucked up the snout.

WATER CHAMELEON

You would think that it would be difficult to find another animal that can compete in colour-changing with the chameleon, but the Seahorse can and does compete well, often matching the weeds it lives in to such degree that it is almost impossible to see.

The male Seahorse spends much of his life in a state of pregnancy.

MALE MOTHERS

Perhaps the Seahorse's most famous claim to fame is the male's ability to get pregnant.

Unlike other baby-carrying males, the Seahorse has a true pregnancy, feeding its young through a placenta, after a gestation that can last between 14 and 28 days, depending on the species.

Like humans, the Seahorse gives birth by contractions, which can last up to 12 hours (no wonder it's the only male in the animal kingdom that does this!).

After this time, the male is exhausted, but he doesn't seem to learn, as he will usually get pregnant again within 48 hours.

The Seahorse can have up to 1,500 young at once (depending on the species) and these are usually born within just a few minutes. Once born, the 5 mm to 8 mm young are on their own, where they will spend up to six weeks swimming in the plankton layer. At this stage, they will settle amongst the algae on the seabed and set up individual territories.

LIFE PARTNERS

Most Seahorse species are believed to pair for life, and the male and female have territories that slightly overlap. Each morning, they will go through an elaborate courtship dance where they reinforce their pair-bonding (page 52).

THREATENED EXISTENCE

Seahorses have long fascinated humankind. Unfortunately, the awe in which we hold the Seahorse, is leading to its downfall. Every year, in excess of 20 million live Seahorses are gathered for the traditional Chinese medicine trade for obscure uses such as 'cures' for menstrual problems, sore throats, baldness, and as aphrodisiacs.

They are also collected to be sold as dried curios such as keyrings, where, mistakenly, most shopkeepers believe the animals have been washed up on the beach after a natural death and then collected. This is not the case: they have been deliberately killed for this appalling trade.

The third trade that is affecting Seahorses is the collection for aquariums as pets or exhibits.

Only people experienced in caring for marine fish should consider keeping Seahorses.

OWNER RESPONSIBILITY

We all have a responsibility, when keeping animals, to give them the best conditions, even if this causes us a great deal of work and expense. If you do not have the time or money, then maybe this is not the hobby for you. This is true of any animal, but is particularly important with regard to more sensitive, demanding species like Seahorses that require a lot of care and attention.

Unless you have had some experience with keeping fish, and, in particular, marine fish, then you should not attempt to keep Seahorses.

In all cases, captive-bred animals should be bought in order to stop the drain on the wild populations. This will also allow the Seahorse-keeper to have a better chance of keeping them alive, as captive-bred animals have invariably been adapted to a non-living captive diet.

Diets are the most difficult part of keeping Seahorses alive and will cause the keeper the most problems and frustrations (page 46). You cannot just feed them once a day with flake food and hope they will survive. An adult Seahorse requires up to 60 live *Mysis* shrimp a day. Since few aquarium shops sell them, most Seahorse keepers have to fish for them in estuaries.

As you can see, keeping Seahorses is a very demanding, time-consuming job!

The best way to conserve Seahorses is to leave them in the wild.

There are a number of ways you can conserve Seahorses:

- Do not buy them as pets unless you can provide for all their needs.

- Swap Seahorses with other fishkeepers or buy only captive-bred animals. Never buy wild-caught specimens.

- Do not buy dead Seahorses from curio shops – they have been deliberately killed to sell to the public.

- Join an organisation such as The Seahorse Trust, in Devon, England, which has been set up to conserve Seahorses.

- Spread the word about the problems Seahorses face in the wild and as pets.

ABSORBING HOBBY

If you are dedicated to caring for the Seahorse and its needs, you cannot wish for a more charming, delightful pet. Beautiful, captivating, and absorbing to watch, your hard work and commitment will be fully rewarded.

CHAPTER 2

CHOOSING SEAHORSES AND TANKMATES

It is estimated that there are about 35 to 40 species of Seahorse in the world, although we are not totally sure, as new species are being found from time to time and the taxonomic classification (the system that is used to identify Seahorses) is still being sorted out.

Your choice of tankmate is more limited, as Seahorses should only share an aquarium with slow-moving, non-competitive species. Suitable fish are described on page 22.

BUYING A SEAHORSE

This confusion about which species is which can lead to Seahorses being wrongly identified in aquarium shops.

Some shops now sell hybrid Seahorses. Pictured: This is a male hybrid.

It is important to check that the Seahorse is healthy and is eating well before you buy it.

Some even sell hybrids (i.e. a cross between two species), so the best way to ensure you get what you want is to contact a private breeder. Ask your local marine fishkeeping club for advice.

Captive-bred animals will survive better in captivity, will be better adapted to a more suitable captive diet, and do not have to go through the stressful journeys that shop-bought ones endure (see page 46). Most people who try to keep Seahorses do so for reasons of conservation. The best way to conserve a species is to leave it in the wild, so if you can buy captive-bred animals then you are doing more for conservation than hoping to breed wild-caught animals.

By dealing with hobbyists, then very often you will have access to free advice and learn from others who have had the trials and tribulations beforehand.

HEALTHY SPECIMENS

When buying Seahorses, the first thing to ascertain is that they are healthy and are eating well.

Look on the Seahorses' snouts and tails for early signs of gas bubble disease, which are small gas bubbles under the skin formed by bacterial gases from wounds on the body. If a Seahorse has them, don't buy it.

Get the supplier to feed the Seahorses. If they respond very slowly or do not eat at all, then do not buy them no matter how sorry you feel for them. It is the responsibility of the supplier to make sure the animals they sell are in good health and are feeding well.

Most importantly, are the Seahorses a good weight? Take a look at the skin between the ridges on the body. If the skin is flush with the ridges, or protrudes just beyond the ridges, then the Seahorse has a good bodyweight. A good place on all Seahorses to check for weight loss are the segments on either side of the neck.

Should the skin sink in, then it is likely that animal is chronically malnourished. The only time that it is acceptable for the skin to sink in, is on the females when they have no eggs stored in their abdomens. If Seahorses are in the latter stages of malnutrition, it will be almost impossible to get them to feed, and they will die.

Do the Seahorses look alert?

Are there any obvious signs of lesions or cuts?

Do their eyes look bright?

Are there any grey patches? (This is often due to a bacterial disease called vibriosis.)

A male Seahorse. A female Seahorse.

IDENTIFYING THE SEX

Males are very easy to identify with their pouch, which hangs below the abdomen. Seahorses are best kept in pairs or groups as this allows for natural behaviour, such as pairing and courtship displays.

POPULAR SPECIES

Below are just some of the more commonly kept species of Seahorse:

BLACK SEAHORSE (*Hippocampus fuscus*)
Distribution: Found in the Indian Ocean around Sri Lanka and India
Size: 4 to 5 inches (10 to 13 cms)
Gestation: 14 to 21 days
No. of young: 100 to 150.

A small Black Seahorse fished in large numbers for the aquarium and Chinese medicine trades. This Seahorse does better than most in captivity, as they adapt better to dead food (although this is not ideal as their only source of food). He lacks the usual Seahorse crown, but has a low crest. Males go pure-white during the courtship display. It likes to have plenty of hiding areas to make it feel secure.

KUDA SEAHORSE (*Hippocampus kuda*)
Distribution: Throughout the tropics
Size: Depends on the Kuda species
Gestation: Between 21 and 28 days, depending on the species
No. of young: From 50 to 250.

A courting pair of Kuda Seahorses (the male is pictured at top).

This is probably the most confusing group of Seahorses in terms of identification. So far, at least ten species have been attributed with the name 'Kuda' (which is Indian for 'big'). They are usually large, coloured Seahorses that commonly are called Giant Caribbean Seahorses, Yellow Seahorses, Giant Seahorses, Coloured Seahorses etc.

PRICKLY SEAHORSE (*Hippocampus histrix*)
Distribution: Indian Ocean
Size: Up to 8 inches (20 to 21 cms)
Gestation: 26 to 28 days.
No. of young: Up to 200.

This usually yellow- to orange-coloured Seahorse has spines (appendages) mainly down its back and on its head. It adapts quicker to captivity than most Seahorses, and will be more likely to take dead food (live food is much better). It can cope well with a moderately-lit tank and prefers a temperature about 78 Fahrenheit (26 Centigrade).

A heavily pregnant Prickly Seahorse male. He gave birth just two hours later.

TIGER TAIL SEAHORSE (*Hippocampus comes*)
Distribution: Philippines and Indonesia
Size: Up to 7 inches (17 to 18 cms from the top of the head to the end of the tail)

Gestation: 24 to 26 days
No. of young: Up to 150.
A striking black Seahorse with yellow bands on the tail.
Healthy Tiger Tail Seahorses have tiny glistening spots
(like tiny jewels) particularly around the head but also
on the body. (All Seahorses should have these spots.)

It is possible that there might be more than one sub-
species of Tiger Tail, due to variance in lengths of the
snout. Supposedly nocturnal, this Seahorse requires
heavy planting in the tank and low light levels.

SPECIES LESS COMMONLY SEEN

Below is a selection of some of the other species, which
are not seen often in aquarium shops:

BIG-BELLIED SEAHORSE (*Hippocampus abdominalis*)
Distribution: Southern Australia
Size: 12 to 14 inches (31 to 36 cms)
Gestation: 28 days
No. of young: Up to 1,500.
This is the largest of all the Seahorse species. It is also
the best swimmer, with a longer dorsal fin than most
Seahorses. They are called the Big-bellied or Pot-bellied
Seahorse, because of the depth of the abdomen, which
gives them the classic 'big belly'.

In the wild, they are known to inhabit algae beds,
but have been seen spending time over sandy bottoms
where they will hunt for shrimp, sitting with their tails
coiled under them like snakes.

Like all Seahorses, they can change colour to blend in
with their surroundings, although they are often a
sandy-beige colour with spots. In captivity, they thrive
in cooler water tanks (68 Fahrenheit; 20 Centigrade).

PACIFIC SEAHORSE (*Hippocampus ingens*)
Distribution: Eastern Pacific, around the Galapagos Islands.
Size: 10 to 12 inches (25 to 31 cms)
Gestation: 27 to 28 days
No. of young: 200 to 300.
This big, bold Seahorse (the second largest Seahorse) typifies the classic Seahorse shape. They have lots of glistening mucus spots all over their body, which gives them the appearance of shining, and they tend to be a steely-grey colour. They are found at a variety of depths and seem to favour the cooler, deeper trenches where the cold upswelling brings ample food, and this should be reflected in captivity (62°F/17°C).

SPINY SEAHORSE (*Hippocampus guttulatus*)
Distribution: Southern and Western British Isles, as high as the Shetland Isles and Ireland. Bay of Biscay, the Mediterranean and the Black Sea.

A mature male Spiny Seahorse, around six years of age.

Size: 6 to 8 inches (15 to 21 cms)
Gestation: 28 days
No. of young: Up to 300.
This is the biggest of the two British species of Seahorse. It is known for its mane of appendages on its head and back, which can be grown or reabsorbed, depending on the animal's camouflage needs. Found mainly in eelgrass beds, it can also live among other types of algae.

Like other temperate Seahorses, they avoid the storms of the winter by going into deeper waters, one individual being recorded at a depth of 254 feet (77.47 metres).

Until relatively recent years, little was known of the British Seahorses. But now the British Seahorse Survey has started to uncover some of the mysteries of the UK's most exotic native fish (see page 2).

SHORT-SNOUTED SEAHORSE
(*Hippocampus hippocampus*)
Distribution: The same as the Spiny Seahorse but also down the African Coast as far as the Cape
Size: 4 to 6 inches (10 to 16 cms)
Gestation: 21 days
No. of young: 150 to 200.
A short, stocky Seahorse often found in a variety

An 18-month-old female Short-snouted Seahorse.

of colours, from purple to orange. Although occupying the same ranges as the Spiny Seahorse, they do not out-compete each other as the Short-snouted Seahorse has adapted differently by having a shorter snout which allows it to target slightly different food types.

GOLDEN SEAHORSE (*Hippocampus whitei*)
Distribution: North and West coasts of Australia, up into Indonesia
Size: 4 to 5 inches (10 to 13 cms) from the top of the head to the end of the tail
Gestation: 14 to 21 days
No. of young: 10 to 150.
A pretty little Seahorse, very often covered in appendages, which gives it a slightly comic, hairy appearance. Usually a light-golden colour, as with all Seahorses they can change to any colour. Unlike other Seahorses that pair for life, however, this Seahorse might be less devoted and have a number of partners. A very gregarious Seahorse and ideal, (if any Seahorse species is 'ideal'), for a first-time Seahorse owner.

PYGMY SEAHORSE (*Hippocampus bargibanti*)
Distribution: Indonesia and the Indian Ocean
Size: 2 inches (5 cms)
Gestation: Not known, but possibly about 14 days
No. of young: Not known, but could be only 10 to 20.
An elusive, very small Seahorse, which lives on Gorgonian Sea Fans in small colonies at a depth of more than 30 feet. Well adapted to its home, this Seahorse resembles the shape and colour of the Sea Fans it lives on. Recent research has shown that there might be more than one species of the Pygmy

Seahorse. At present, this species is rarely, if ever, seen in captivity.

KNYSNA SEAHORSE (*Hippocampus capensis*)
Distribution: Knysna Estuary, Svartveli Estuary, and Kerbooms Estuary in South Africa
Size: 4 to 5 inches (10 to 13 cms)
Gestation: 21 days
No. of young: 50 to 300
The Knysna Seahorse is now very rare and has full protection in South Africa. It has a crest and is usually pale-beige with black or grey spots. Living in the Knysna Lagoons, it tolerates a wide range of salinities due to flash-flooding bringing lots of fresh water through the lagoons. Not usually available to private Seahorse keepers.

A year-old male Knysna Seahorse.

Seahorses are better suited to life with their own kind, or with other, slow-moving, non-competitive species, such as these Pipefish (right).

SELECTING TANKMATES

Seahorses are a slow-moving, highly-specialised predator, an opportunistic hunter that waits for food to swim past and then grabs it. Because of the nature of the beast, they cannot compete with fast-moving fish for food and suffer badly at the hands of much stronger, quicker fish that can be bullies. As a result of this, Seahorses are much better off in a species-only tank or with non-competitive tank companions (mixing different species could result in hybridization, so is not advised).

A golden rule when thinking about other species to put into the Seahorse tank is: choose slow, non-competitive species, and, if in any doubt, don't do it.

Seahorses are fascinating in their own right and don't need other species in the tank.

SHRIMPS

Feeding is crucial in keeping Seahorses, due to their digestive system that is poorly developed and which results in them eating large quantities of food. Because of this, you will need to put large quantities of food into the tank, which, in effect, can be quite polluting without the help of a 'cleaning crew' in the tank.

One of the best cleaners for a Seahorse tank is the Hump-backed or Common Cleaner Shrimp (*Lysmata amboinensis*), which is a striking red-and-pale-yellow-coloured shrimp that will happily live together in groups and with the Seahorses. They can often be seen sitting on the Seahorse, cleaning it of flakes of skin and parasites.

Another striking and useful shrimp for the Seahorse tank is the Fire or Blood Shrimp (*Lysmata debelius*), which is blood-red in colour and is usually better kept as pairs.

Most of the shrimp species are ideal tank companions for Seahorses and do a good job in cleaning the tank as well. Quite often they are as interesting as the Seahorses in their behaviour.

HERMIT CRABS

Hermit crabs make good companions for Seahorses as long as they are not too large (they have been known to attack the less active Seahorse) and their antics will keep you amused for hours (be sure to put in extra shells to allow them to change homes occasionally).

MANDARIN FISH

Once your tank has been established for a while to allow a build-up of copepods (small crustaceans) in the

tank, then you could think about adding a Mandarin
fish (*Pterosynchiropus splendidus*). These small-mouthed,
brilliantly-coloured bottom dwellers are a gentle fish to
other tank companions, but should be kept individually,
as they will fight to the death if you put two males in
together. They are fascinating to watch, as they pick the
copepods off the rocks in the tank and will scavenge the
bottom of the tank.

PIPEFISH

One of the best companions to put into a Seahorse
tank are their close relatives, the Pipefish. They often
share the same food as Seahorses and have the same
water requirements. An added advantage is that they
are very similar to the Seahorses, and some will swim in
mid-water so they are often on view.

A close
relation of the
Seahorse, the
Pipefish makes
an ideal
tankmate.

CHAPTER 3

A SEAHORSE HOME

Choosing the right tank for a Seahorse is crucial. They require both base area and height, so a square tank is the best design, preferably at least 2 feet cubed (60 cms³) for one pair of Seahorses. If you are looking at a more traditional shape, then make sure the tank is at least as high as the depth from front to back.

SPACIOUS ACCOMMODATION

Seahorses are territorial in the wild and they use every part of it. This is the same in the Seahorse aquarium, so they need as much room as possible to move around the whole of the tank. It is a long-held myth that Seahorses do not need much room because they appear not to move much. If you watch Seahorses over a 24-hour period, you will be surprised at how much they travel around their tank. Having a lot of room in the tank will allow you to create plenty of hiding areas. This is essential, as Seahorses are, in essence, shy animals and they relish their space.

Seahorses need a tank that has sufficient height to allow them to climb.

Seahorses are very shy animals that require plenty of hiding places. Pictured: Juvenile Spiny Seahorses.

For an animal that spends its life as benthic (seabed living), it might seem strange to suggest they need plenty of height in their tank. This allows for holdfasts at all water-depths in the tank. Not only does this allow them an opportunity to climb around in search of food, but it is primarily for the courtship displays. These focus around an object on the seabed, but culminates in the Seahorse swimming up into the water column. (See Chapter Eight: Courtship and Breeding.)

TANK SHAPE AND ACCESSIBILITY

There are a number of unusual-shaped tanks on the market and it doesn't matter whether the tank is glass or acrylic. What is very important is access to keep the tank clean. Like all animals, Seahorses need to have their environment kept very clean to prevent disease build-up, so a tank that is awkward to get into or which is difficult to maintain, should be avoided.

Bear in mind also, that acrylic tanks can become very scratched after a short while if care is not taken when cleaning the tank. The advantage of acrylic tanks, however, is that they allow some interesting-shaped tanks to be formed, although, on the whole, they tend to be more expensive.

TANK STAND

It is important to think about the stand for the tank and the weight. Water weighs 10 lbs for every gallon (4.53 kilos per 4.55 litres), so the more water you have, the heavier the tank. There are a number of questions you need to ask about the positioning of the tank. How heavy will it be? Will the stand take the weight? Will the floor take the weight? (A concrete floor is far better for large fish tanks.)

Remember, it is not just the water that weighs a lot; if you are using rockwork and substrates in the tank, these will add to the overall weight. Just a tip: do not place the tank in direct sunlight, as this will increase algae in the tank and you will need to clean it off every day. You will also have problems with fluctuating temperatures.

TANK FURNISHING AND DECOR

In furnishing the tank, height is also very important. Hiding places are vital to Seahorses to give them a sense of security. It might be supposed that by giving so many hiding places, the Seahorses will never be seen, but, in fact, it is the opposite that happens. The more secure a Seahorse feels, the more relaxed it will be, and the more it will venture out and about in its tank.

Seahorses use their tails to climb plants around the tank.

ESSENTIAL ALGAE

By building up the rockwork of a tank, it will allow you to plant the algae at all levels. This gives a tumbling effect in the algae, which is not only decorative, but is also ideal for Seahorses to climb around on. It is surprising how similar Seahorses are to monkeys. Being poor swimmers, they will actively use their tails to 'climb' algae or objects. The denser the algae, the better the environment for the Seahorses, again for their sense of security.

These algae have two added advantages. Firstly, they provide the vital holdfasts; secondly, the *Caulerpa* algae, in particular, help to remove nitrate wastes from the water.

LIVING ROCK

Living rock (rock that has been colonised by living animals and algae) from a sustainable source is ideal as a basis for the Seahorse tank, as it will come with a number of species of algae growing from it or seeded in it.

Some living rock is taken from ecologically sensitive areas with little or no regard as to the environmental consequences. Check with your shop as to the source of the rock; if they do not know the answers, then get them to find out. We all have a responsibility as marine fishkeepers to make sure we are not devastating the wild just for our hobby. If possible, swap living rock with other marine keepers.

Be very careful that the many anemones that also grow on the living rock do not get out of hand or too large, as they will sting Seahorses and cause various skin problems, possibly leading to death. With some of the larger anemones, they will even capture and consume the relatively slow-moving Seahorses that do not have the speed and swimming strength to get away.

DRIFTWOOD

Other holdfasts can be created by using wood. When on a trip to the seaside, driftwood can be collected from the beach. The advantage of this is that the wood has been 'bleached' by the sea, and also it is smoother for the Seahorses to hold on to.

A word of caution: some areas of the beach can have oil or tar on them, so be careful that anything you collect from the seaside is clean and non-polluting.

For ecological reasons, Seafans should not be purchased.

SEA FANS

Sea Fans, a beautiful fan-shaped colony of animals that, when dead, leave behind a fan-shaped skeleton, should be avoided for Seahorses. Most of them have been targeted by collectors for the aquarium trade, often with dire consequences for the Sea Fans themselves (which were alive before collection) and the area around them. Corals are suffering the same fate, so ethically should not be used.

The second reason not to use them is their fine, meshed structure. Most Seahorses prefer to hold on to large smooth objects (the uplift tubes of the undergravel filter are a favourite), so the thin Sea Fans are not adequate. If they are the only source of holdfast in the tank, the Seahorse will become unsettled as it cannot relax.

CHAPTER
4

WATER QUALITY

W hen designing the layout of the tank, a lot of
thought must be given to the type of filtration and
saltwater to be used. The author highly recommends
natural seawater from a good clean source for Seahorses.
As many people live less than 100 miles away from the
sea, this is not as difficult as it sounds. It can be collected
in large buckets with lids on. Make sure it matches the
temperature of the tank water before you put it in the
tank.

SEAWATER QUALITY
A good way of ascertaining the water quality of an area
from which you intend to collect is to watch the fish and
other marine life. If it is lively and there appears to be lots
of creatures swimming around with no signs of lesions or
other damage to their bodies, then it is a good sign that
all is well. Plenty of invertebrates are always a good sign.

However, you should take other precautions as well,
such as testing the water quality for all the usual
parameters, such as ammonia, nitrite, nitrate and salinity.
Water test kits can be bought from your local aquarium
supplier, and, provided you follow the manufacturer's
instructions, they are very accurate.

For more detailed information on filtration and water
chemistry, see *Filtration and Water Chemistry* (a title in the
Practical Fishkeeping series), by Dr. Peter Burgess.

ARTIFICIAL SEAWATER

If it is not possible to use natural seawater, then artificial seawater can be used. It is worth paying for a good-quality product and you should follow the instructions closely. A good rule of thumb with Seahorses is to do frequent, small water changes, as they do not like sudden big changes.

There are a couple of obvious differences between natural and artificial seawater, and one of them is cost. Using artificial seawater can become

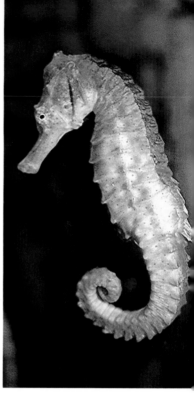

Natural seawater is infinitely better than artificial alternatives.

costly, especially when you start to breed Seahorses, which will mean using large quantities of water. However, for those Seahorse-keepers who live a long way from the sea, transporting seawater can be equally expensive.

The main difference, though, is that magic sparkle that natural seawater gives to fish. The author has used natural seawater with corals, Seahorses and other marine fish, and the results, as long as the precautions recommended are followed, are usually much better and more spectacular than the artificial equivalent.

FILTRATION

The adage 'keep it simple' should be the rule with
Seahorses, and this applies to the filtration as well.
There are a large number of filtration systems on the
market. Some of them are extremely good, but others
are basically just gimmicks which take simple systems
and wrap them up in a complex package that are prone
to going wrong or breaking down.

UNDERGRAVEL FILTER

A much underestimated but well-tried filtration system
is the undergravel filter. Like some of the more complex
filters, the undergravel filter is a biological filter (it
harbours friendly bacteria that break down the fish's
waters). If maintained properly, it will perform well
year after year.

Once matured in the Seahorse tank where the
biological load (i.e. the amount of living matter in the
tank) is low, it will prove to be a very efficient, and,
compared with its more complex cousins, is a relatively
easy filter to maintain.

To maintain the undergravel filter, it should not be
allowed to clog up with particulate matter, as this will
impede the movement of water through the substrate,
leading to undesirable
anaerobic areas (areas that
have no oxygen in them).
So once a week when you
are doing your water
changes (20 per cent per
week is recommended),
use a siphon to remove
excess dirt from the gravel.

Undergravel filters
are reliable and
easy to maintain.

A length of plastic siphon tubing can be bought quite cheaply from the aquarium shop and is easy to use (after a couple of mouthfuls of dirty tank water, you soon learn how to do it). There is even a self-priming type that means you don't have to suck the pipe to get the siphon started.

When siphoning the muck from the gravel, allow the water and muck to go into a bucket and then pour it away to waste. This will mean that you are doing water changes and gravel siphoning at the same time.

Once this has been done, then top the tank up with new seawater. This should be the same temperature as the tank water to avoid sudden temperature changes that can lead to shock and ultimately death. Also check that it is matched for salinity.

SUBSTRATE

By having undergravel filtration, it gives you quite a choice of substrates for the tank (e.g coarse sand or pea gravel). If it is possible to get hold of some matured filter medium from another tank, this will quicken the maturation process in the Seahorse tank, but be sure first that the tank it comes from is disease free.

A tip for getting sterile substrate to mature quickly is to put a small amount of fish food e.g. a couple of dead *Mysis* shrimps. into the tank on a daily basis. This should be done before putting any fish into the tank.

Be sure to remove and replenish it daily. This will allow the filter medium to go through the ammonia cycle before the introduction of fish. This process should only take a couple of weeks.

When introducing your fish be sure that it is done a

couple at a time to allow the filter to cope with the increases in biological load.

In setting up the undergravel filter, do not use very fine substrates as these can clog the filter (layering – fine sand above coarse – doesn't work for long: eventually, the fine substrate settles down and blocks the filter).

Make sure all substrates are thoroughly washed before being put into the tank. The better the flow of water through the substrate, the better the filter, so the water should be drawn through the uplift tubes either by a powerful air pump or motorised water pumps (power heads) on to the uplift tubes. An airline needs to be put into the tank if a powerhead is used.

It is important that the substrate is partially cleaned weekly (be careful not to overclean the substrate or you could remove all the helpful bacteria), and this can easily be achieved by siphoning the muck out of the gravel during the weekly water change. This has the added effect of stirring the gravel, which keeps it from compacting.

The substrate should be washed thoroughly before being placed in the tank.

CANISTER FILTER

Its a good idea to install a canister filter in addition to the undergravel one. Canister filters also work biologically and have the advantage of removing particulate matter from the water. The outflow of the canister filter also creates a current of water around the tank, which is ideal for Seahorses and the algae in the tank.

A canister filter will remove large particles from the water and will provide currents for the Seahorses to swim in.

Water movement is crucial for Seahorses when you think of the areas they live in the wild. Some species live in shallow, weedy areas with strong currents; others live in very turbulent conditions. By changing the direction of the flow periodically (e.g. by adjusting the position of the canister filter's outflow pipe), it will stop any repetitive, stereotypic behaviour. It is surprising how strong a current a Seahorse likes, and it is worth experimenting with flows and directions to get the best results.

OTHER FILTERS

As well as conventional undergravel and canister filters, there are a number of others on the market and some are better than others. When deciding which you would like to try, have a word with other fishkeepers and see what their preference is, and ask them which products they have had difficulties with.

Some filters are much more complex than they need to be; this is to convince the buyer that the product is a much better filter. Just beware of gimmicks, as these usually cost the most and boast the most.

There has been a move towards more natural filtration in recent years, such as the 'algae scrubbers' (a natural process which removes nitrates and nitrites from the water). These are excellent, but take lots of room.

It is worth looking around and doing some research before you decide on a filter.

WATER PARAMETERS

Seahorses come from all over the world, and, because of this, they vary from species to species as to their water parameters (the optimum conditions for the chemistry or make up of the water).

Although most species of Seahorse available for the aquarium trade come from full saltwater conditions, there are some Seahorses that live all or part of their lives in brackish water and there is even one species which is supposed to come from freshwater (although this is widely argued amongst Seahorse experts).

When you buy a Seahorse, it is important that you ascertain what water conditions it requires.

As with all fish species, it is important to keep
ammonia and nitrite levels at or near zero, and to
maintain a low nitrate level. With the temperature,
specific gravity (the amount of salts dissolved into the
water) and pH (the acidity of the water, from acid to
alkaline), this will vary as to where the species of
Seahorse comes from.

Listed below are some examples of extremes between
Seahorse species. You should research the species of
Seahorse you intend to buy, especially with specific
regard to where it comes from. You can then match the
water conditions.

Tiger Tail Seahorses *(Hippocampus comes)*

Distribution:	Indian Ocean
Temperature:	25 to 26 Centigrade (77 to 78 Fahrenheit)
Specific gravity:	35ppt
pH:	8.2

Spiny Seahorse *(Hippocampus guttulatus)*

Distribution:	Western Atlantic (British Isles), Bay of Biscay, Mediterranean
Temperature:	16 to 19 Centigrade (60 to 66 Fahrenheit), depending on the time of year.
Specific gravity:	31 to 32ppt
pH:	7.5 to 7.9

Knysna Seahorse *(Hippocampus capensis)*

Distribution:	Knysna, Swartvlei, and Keurbooms Lagoons in South Africa
Temperature:	20 to 26 Centigrade (68 to 78 Fahrenheit) depending on time of year.
pH:	6 to 8.3. This is dependent on the freshwater washing through their lagoons in the wild, but in captivity an optimum of 7.8 to 7.9 is advisable.

CHAPTER
5

LIGHTING UP

Lighting is a matter of compromises. Seahorses like low light levels, similar to their wild conditions, where they hide out of direct sunlight or lurk amongst weeds and algae which shelter them. There is at least one species of Seahorse, the Tiger Tail Seahorse (*Hippocampus comes*), that is thought to be nocturnal. Conversely, a Seahorse aquarium needs a good growth of algae and, obviously, you want to be able to see the Seahorses, so you will need a good light source.

The Tiger Tail is thought to be a nocturnal species of Seahorse.

EXPERIMENT

Experiment with different arrangements of lights to see what effects you can create. However, the Seahorses' needs must be paramount, as they are not tolerant of the type of bright lighting used for coral tanks, unless they have plenty of areas to hide in.

SPOTLIGHT

A good way of getting over this problem is to illuminate just part of the tank with spotlights, enabling the Seahorse to retreat to the shadiest area if it so wishes. As well as the shafts of light being aesthetically pleasing, it will create luxuriant growth for the Seahorses to get into if they wish.

Although the rest of the tank will be darker than the areas with the shafts of light, you will still be able to see the aquarium clearly and relatively brightly due to the refraction of the light in the water.

FLUORESCENT TUBE

Another way of lighting your Seahorse tank is to have one fluorescent tube running along the front. (A second one with a blue light across the back will give a blue glow, which will not upset the Seahorses.) This will create a very light area along the front and a lower light level area in the back of the tank.

Although not as aesthetically pleasing as the spotlights, the tubes give the advantage of illuminating a larger area for the growing of the algae.

One of the best tubes the author has used is a 'life glo' tube, designed for growing plants, and which is ideal for growing marine algae, such as the *Caulerpa*. (See Chapter Five: Lighting Up.)

Seahorses prefer low-level lighting, and will become stressed if conditions are too bright.

DIMMER SWITCH

When deciding on your lighting regime, consider using dimmer switches (unfortunately these cannot be used with fluorescent tubes). A dimmer switch will allow you to increase and decrease the light levels more slowly. This is much better for any marine fish, but in particular the Seahorse.

Another option is to use several non-connected light sources which will allow you to turn them off independently, and, in consequence, to lower or to raise the light levels accordingly.

LIGHT STRESS

Seahorses are very susceptible to stress and one of the most extreme forms of stress can be caused by a brightly-lit tank. Having said this, if there is sufficient areas for the Seahorse to either hide away in, or to be comfortable in, then they will be very relaxed and will venture around the tank without regard to the brightness of the light.

A brighty-lit tank, with few hiding places, causes considerable distress.

PHOTOPERIOD

Like all animals, Seahorses require a certain period of light in each day. A minimal length of time to have the tank lights on would be eight hours. A photoperiod is the natural sequence of lighting in a 24-hour period including night and day.

To create a more natural photoperiod, you should find out where your Seahorses come from in the wild and try to match the lighting as near as possible. If your Seahorses come from the equator, the day and night lengths will be 12 hours light and 12 hours dark. As you go further north or south, the length of day and night will change with different times of year. For instance, the British Seahorses will have a maximum daylight in the winter of 6 to 7 hours and up to 15 hours in the summer. Sometimes, the correct day length can make all the difference if you are trying to breed animals of all kinds.

CHAPTER

6

PLANTING THE TANK

The next step is to think about the soft landscaping (i.e. marine plants) of the tank. When doing this, the main objective should be to create a home for the Seahorses in your care.

Planting the tank is vital for the welfare of the Seahorses. It should both look good and allow the Seahorses to have a more secure environment.

When arranging the rockwork, create areas that enable the Seahorses to hide out of sight from each other. This is necessary because they have excellent eyesight and the constant strain of seeing a rival will cause them stress.

Carefully-designed rockwork and planting will ensure that rival Seahorses can hide from each other, and feel secure in their environment.

Caulerpa taxifolia (pictured) is an ideal plant for the Seahorse aquarium.

ALGAE

With the rocks in place, the algae can then be placed in suitable spots around the tank. The more algae in the tank, the better it will look, but it is doing more than just looking good: it also acts as a holdfast, and filters the harmful nitrates out of the water in the same fashion as an algal scrubber filter would do.

One of the fastest growing group of algae are the *Caulerpa*, two of the most common found in aquariums are *Caulerpa taxifolia* and *Caulerpa prolifera* – both are ideal Seahorse plants, due to the speed of growth and the dense cover they provide. They can be bought from a good marine aquarium stockist.

They normally get to the point where they have to be cut back severely due to overgrowth. This allows you to swap plants with fellow aquarists (a word of caution: check any incoming plants and algae for unwanted visitors, such as *Aiptasia* anemones). It will help to increase the growth of these algae if they are cut back periodically, as this will stimulate them into spurts of growth.

SEEDING

A second, more pressing, reason to cut the *Caulerpa* back is to stop them from seeding. Seeding occurs periodically and can have devastating results to the marine aquarium.

The *Caulerpa* starts to go a light grey colour just prior to seeding and will then dump all its seeds into the tank of the water, causing the water to go cloudy, and may even kill certain fish. Although Seahorses won't die if the *Caulerpa* seeds, they can become stressed if the water deteriorates as a result.

Should seeding take place, a large water change is needed immediately and should be repeated until the water is clear again. After seeding, the *Caulerpa* dies off and should be removed.

A plus point of the seeding is that, in the soft tissue of wood or some of the softer rocks, the *Caulerpa* seedlings will sprout out quite quickly and this will increase the growth in the tank.

Due to its dense nature, the *Caulerpa* is also ideal from a holdfast point of view as, despite being soft, the Seahorse can grip it well.

EEL GRASSES

Experiment with planting your tank with a variety of plants and algae. You could also attempt to recreate an eelgrass bed in the tank by using one of the tropical or sub-tropical eelgrasses or similar, such as turtle grass, *Thalassia testudinum*.

To do this, you will need to create a strong flow of water through the tank. You should keep a close eye on hair algae that will smother the eelgrass and stop it from photosynthesising.

THE RIGHT DIET

Feeding is the most difficult part of keeping Seahorses in an aquarium.

LIVE FOODS

Good-quality live foods, such as *Mysis* shrimp, will allow you to have a healthy, well-fed animal. An adult Seahorse should eat in the region of 50 to 60 full size (about 1 inch or 2.5 cm) *Mysis* shrimp per day.

Poor feeding regimes and high stress levels are responsible for the majority of premature Seahorse deaths during transportation.

A healthy adult Seahorse will eat around 60 Mysis shrimp each day.

FISHING FOR FOOD

Unfortunately, very few aquarium shops sell *Mysis* shrimp, so the only way to get them is by fishing for them in muddy estuaries. You can stand on the side of the estuary and use a long-handled net to scoop up the shrimp, but, during the winter, this can be a long process as the shrimp sink to the bottom of the estuary in cooler periods.

River shrimp can be fed to Seahorses as a nutritional alternative to *Mysis* shrimp. Pictured: a pair of mature Pacific Seahorses.

When transporting the *Mysis* shrimp, take a battery-powered air pump to aerate the water, as they may die if the oxygen level in the water becomes low.

Another good source of food is river shrimp, and these can be collected in the same way as the *Mysis* shrimp. The shrimps are also available at good aquarium shops.

Feeding adult live brine shrimp (*Artemia*) is another option, though less satisfying for the Seahorses. The shrimp should be fed together with a good-quality algae-based enrichment (available from retail outlets).

Frozen algae should be soaked in enrichment and then re-frozen. You can buy brine shrimp, in dried cyst (egg) form, from aquarium shops, but follow the instructions on the pack very closely to hatch them and to grow them. Some aquarium shops sell brine shrimp as adults.

Out of choice, Seahorses will feed on *Mysis* shrimp.

DEAD FOOD

It is possible to train Seahorses to feed on dead food, such as frozen *Mysis* which has not thawed from frozen (thawed shrimp lose much of its nutritional value in the process of thawing), but it takes time and you have to have healthy animals in the first place.

Seahorses can be trained to eat frozen food, but live food is preferred.

It is done by placing the dead, frozen shrimp in the flow of the filter and allowing it to be powered around the tank; this should stimulate the Seahorse into following it, thinking that it is alive. If you are lucky, it will then try to eat it. Some Seahorses will take to dead food quite quickly, but others take weeks to adapt.

Dead food will have to be enriched with an algae-based food supplement (see page 49) before it is fed because the lost nutritional value has to be replaced.

Several meals are needed throughout the day as Seahorses cannot retain food in their digestive system for long periods of time.

A nutritious
diet produces
healthy,
happy
Seahorses.

NUMBER OF MEALS

Seahorse digestion is very simple. Seahorses do not
have a true stomach, so food is not retained for any
length of time in the body. This is the main reason that
Seahorses need to feed throughout the day.

   If you are using dead food, the Seahorses will need to
be fed three to four times a day. If feeding live food, it
should be in the tank with the Seahorses all the time.

CHAPTER
8

COURTSHIP AND BREEDING

Once Seahorses have paired, and if they are in reasonably good health, then most will breed. This will then become the most challenging part of keeping Seahorses (next to feeding). With anywhere from 10 to 1,500 babies born, depending on the species, and with the fry (babies) eating up to 3,000 particles of food a day, this is a major undertaking.

However, the importance of breeding cannot be underestimated – if more aquarists can breed Seahorses, then the pressure on the wild populations will diminish.

COURTSHIP DANCES

Most Seahorse species pair for life, with territories of the male and female overlapping each other in the wild. Males have about 6 square feet (1.83 square metres) for their territory, and females 15 square feet (4.58 square metres). Once paired, they will reinforce this bonding each day with a courtship dance. Usually done first thing in the morning, the male will seek out the female, either by looking for her or by sending out a chemical message in the form of pheromones into the water. Once she has sensed these, she will find the male.

The dance centres around an object on the seabed, where the male will circle the female in what can only be described as a shimmering dance. He will stiffen his body with his chin on his chest, and, as he changes

The daily courtship dance between Seahorse couples is both enchanting and endearing. Pictured: male (left) and female (right) in a courtship display.

colour, he will circle the female. In response, she will circle with him, matching his colour and copying his body posture. Most days, the dance will last anywhere from 30 minutes to an hour, sometimes more.

THE 'MATING'

Once the male has produced a batch of fry then the following morning or within the next couple of days the courtship display takes on a different intensity. Instead of them just separating at the end of the display, the male and female will repeatedly rise together in the water column. They will mimic each other's movements with the lead being taken by the male.

In the Big Bellied Seahorse, as with some other species, they will lift their heads simultaneously together; this rising will happen a number of times before the synchronisation is just right.

The male can carry between 10 and 1,500 eggs in his brood pouch. Pictured: a heavily pregnant male Golden Seapony.

The male and female face each other at the top of their rise in the water and the female will then put her ovipositor into the male's pouch, depositing between 10 and 1,500 orange eggs (depending on the species). At this point, they both separate and go their separate ways to meet again the following morning for the daily courtship dance.

FERTILIZED EGGS

With a pouch full of eggs, the male goes to the seabed, and, with a lot of wriggling, self-fertilizes the eggs that are embedding into the lining of the pouch. This done, he goes about his business with the usual calm and tranquillity that Seahorses have. The fertilized eggs are fed partly through the placental lining of the pouch and partly by the yolk reserves within the eggs.

THE BIRTH

The male's tranquil life comes to an end 14 to 28 days later, when he goes into contractions ready for giving birth. These contractions can last up to 12 hours until he gives birth, in just a few seconds producing a cloud of perfect miniature replicas.

NEWBORN FRY

The fry (babies) are completely independant when they are born. In the wild, they spend much of the first six to eight weeks swimming in the plankton layer, eating. They can each consume up to 3,000 particles of food per day and this is one of the main problems facing breeders. Trying to replicate this amount of food in captivity is not easy, and, to add to the problems, it has to be highly nutritious and relatively soft in texture due to the Seahorse's poor digestive system.

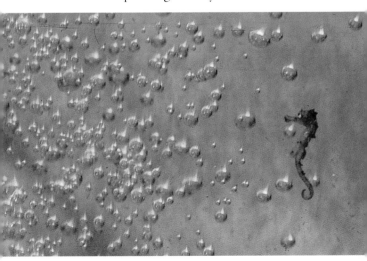

A five-day-old male Golden Seapony, measuring just 7 mm from head to tail tip.

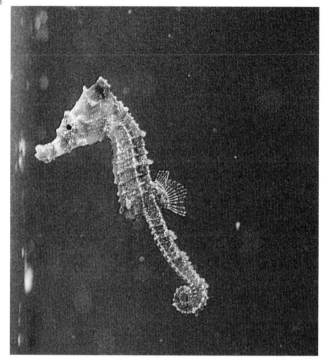

Fry are miniature replicas of adult Seahorses. Pictured: three-week-old fry, measuring around $2^1/_2$ inches (6.5cms).

It is best to separate the newborn fry from the adults so that the feeding and water quality can more easily be controlled. It is pointless to try to keep all the fry, due to the feeding problems, so select 20 of the strongest-looking fry and concentrate on them (the remaining fry can be left in the tank with the adults for nature to take its course).

This might seem cruel, but you will see as you read on about the food difficulties associated with feeding Seahorse fry. As your experience builds up, try to replicate more fry food and rear more Seahorse fry.

FRY FOODS

One of the most commonly-used foods for Seahorse fry are *Artemia* nauplii (newly-hatched Brine Shrimp), although it is worth experimenting with all types of foods, such as Rotifers, *Mysis* nauplii etc.

ARTEMIA

If hatching *Artemia* cysts, then set up three pots with airlines in them at least three different times of the day (although five times a day would be much, much better).

It is important to feed freshly-hatched food several times throughout the day because, during the first five to six days, the Seahorse fry have difficulty digesting the hard carapace (shell) on older *Artemia* nauplii.

Even a delay of two hours between hatching and feeding will make the *Artemia* nauplii less digestible to the Seahorse fry.

To remove the *Artemia* nauplii from the hatching pots, take the airline out of the pot and let the water settle down.

The nauplii will swim to the bottom of the pot (you can use a strong light to attract them downwards), and the egg shells will float to the top.

When this separation is complete, siphon the shrimp from the bottom of the pot into a net and then wash it clean under fresh water. You can then feed it to the fry.

It is important to feed just enough to be cleared by the Seahorse fry by the time the next feed is due (with experience, you will learn how much to put in).

This will stop any *Artemia* staying in the tank and developing to too large a size, and will also minimise the risk of pollution.

Older fry require considerable nourishment. This tank is home to six-week-old juveniles.

MYSIS

One of the many problems with Seahorse fry is the lack of special bacteria in their gut to digest the food. By putting scrapings of dead *Mysis* in the tank on a daily basis, this will encourage a bacterial 'soup' which will be ingested by the fry. This, in turn, will aid the digestive process.

It is vital to replenish this daily by removing the old *Mysis* bodies and putting in new to stop pollution problems. Putting dead *Mysis* in the tank from day one also helps with training your Seahorses to eat dead food as they get older. Dead food is not an ideal food, but is better than some foods that are on offer. As successive generations of Seahorses survive, their ability to deal with poor foods such as dead shrimp is better. So if you can get captive-bred Seahorses, then you stand a better chance of success.

OLDER FRY

As the Seahorses get older (weeks four to six), the amount they are eating is enormous compared with the nutritional value they get from it, so a bigger, better-quality food needs to be found.

There are a number of options, such as growing the *Artemia* to a larger stage and enriching it with algae or an equally good additive (*Artemia* can be enriched by putting enrichment into the water and they will eat it.)

Another option is to collect a larger food type, such as live juvenile *Mysis* shrimps. You will need to set up a separate tank to house the adult *Mysis* shrimps, and, as they give birth, collect the shrimp larvae and feed them to the Seahorse fry.

There are a number of problems using this system, the first of which is collecting the adult *Mysis*. These can be collected from estuaries, but, at certain times of the year (winter and early spring), are in very low numbers. The second problem is getting enough to feed the Seahorse fry.

WATER QUALITY

Water quality can be a major problem with Seahorse fry, so filtering the water or changing the water frequently is very important. The filter in a fry tank should be a sponge filter.

A tip: make sure the Seahorse fry tank is kept scrupulously clean, as one of the biggest killers of Seahorse fry is disease, which thrives in dirty conditions.

HEALTH MATTERS

To keep healthy Seahorses, feed them on good-quality live food, make sure their water quality is of the highest standard, keep the tank clean, and avoid stressful surroundings. Good husbandry is a basic necessity for any animal, but with Seahorses, with their very specific needs, it is vital.

Seahorses are susceptible to all the usual fish diseases (see *Common Fish Ailments*, by Dr. Peter Burgess, in this *Practical Fishkeeping* series); however, the following ailments are particularly common.

It is your responsibility to create a healthy environment for your Seahorses.

GAS BUBBLE DISEASE

This can affect Seahorses in two ways: in the male's pouch or under its skin (on the snout or in the tail region). In exceptional cases, it can appear all over the body. Both are thought to be caused by bacterial gases.

POUCH TYPE

The pouch type of Gas Bubble Disease is caused by decaying embryos or fry that have died in the pouch. When this happens, the pouch fills with gas, causing floatation problems. If left untreated, the Seahorse will die of starvation or stress.

Gas bubbles in the pouch are detected by the seahorse floating, and the presence of a large abnormal swelling in the pouch. Gas under the skin again causes floating and also large lumps under the skin.

Removing the gas requires very gentle but firm handling of the Seahorse under the water. Hold the Seahorse in one hand, and, with a fine, open pipette (i.e. without a teat fitted), insert it by angling downwards into the opening of the pouch (at the top

Keeping Seahorses is not easy, as they suffer from a number of specific problems.

of the pouch). Under no circumstances should cocktails sticks or similar be used. Slowly twist as the pipette is pushed in. Be careful not to push in too far, as you will damage the pouch internally. Once in the pouch, you will notice gas escaping through the pipette.

The next stage is to flush the pouch, via the pipette, with an antibiotic and antibacterial mix. There are a number of good types on the market, but be sure to follow the correct directions on the packet (in Britain, you will need a veterinary certificate).

It is easiest to flush the pouch with a small fine-nozzled hand-held spray bottle down the pipette. After flushing with the antibacterial mix, flush with clean sea-water which is the same temperature as the tank water. Do this several times and repeat for two to three days.

SKIN VARIETY

The Gas Bubble under the skin is more difficult to deal with, as the bubbles need lancing with a sterilized surgical pin or needle (the finer the better). The wound would then need to be treated with a topical anti-bacterial ointment. If in doubt, contact your vet.

BACTERIAL PROBLEMS

Infections such as caused by *Vibrio* bacteria are probably the biggest killer of Seahorses (apart from stress). This is mainly because we know very little about them, and because they are so virulent. Unfortunately, most of these problems result in death.

The first obvious signs are small grey patches on the body. As soon as they are seen, separate the affected Seahorse into an isolation tank, as the condition is potentially highly contagious.

Bacterial problems are often fatal in a Seahorse aquarium.

To treat the Seahorse, it will need to be handled out of water (be very careful). Dry the infected area with a tissue and apply an antibacterial solution to the area. It will then need covering with Vaseline (petroleum jelly) or similar to stop it washing off. Be sure to have all you need at hand and do the treatment very quickly.

Another way of dealing with some strains of *Vibrio* bacteria is to lower the temperature (slowly) in the isolation tank to stem the spread of the disease. The temperature can be dropped by either lowering the thermostat every hour by two degrees C or by turning it off. This is because *Vibrio* may be more harmful in warm water. Be sure to keep an eye on the Seahorse to stop it from stressing. Increase the temperature again if it is showing any signs of stress or stops feeding. Once the grey patches disappear, you can slowly increase the temperature again back to the normal temperature.

STRESS

Being a highly sensitive animal, the Seahorse is likely to go into stress at any point, so the secret is not to stress it in the first place. A stressed state will make the Seahorse more susceptible to diseases. Listed below are a number of ways to minimise stress:

STRESS BUSTERS
- Raise and lower light levels slowly
- Keep them in species-only tanks or with compatible tank companions
- Provide active stimulants like live food
- Feed the correct foods
- Make sure they have plenty of cover in the tank
- Keep in pairs not in male-only tanks
- Place the tank in a quiet area, with little movement outside of the tank
- Provide good, clean water and do not allow the water to deteriorate
- When doing water changes, make sure they are frequent small changes (about 15 to 20 per cent each week) and not infrequent large changes.

SUMMARY

Delicate, beautiful and quite unlike any other fish, the Seahorse has fascinated people for centuries. Owning such an unusual animal requires a full-time commitment (in terms of time and money), but your efforts will be rewarded with the privilege of being able to watch these mysterious creatures up-close, and sharing their peace and tranquillity.